NEW BELIEVER'S GUIDE TO
the Bible

New Believer's®
GUIDE TO
THE BIBLE

GREG LAURIE

TYNDALE HOUSE PUBLISHERS, INC.
WHEATON, ILLINOIS

Visit Tyndale's exciting Web site at www.tyndale.com

New Believer's Guide to the Bible

Library of Congress Cataloging-in-Publication Data

Laurie, Greg.
  New believer's guide to the Bible / Greg Laurie ; with Linda Taylor.
    p. cm.
Includes bibliographical references.
ISBN 0-8423-5573-1 (pbk.)
1. Bible—Introductions.   I. Taylor, Linda Chaffee, 1958-   II. Title.

BS475.3 .L38 2003
220.6′1—dc21   2002015183

Printed in the United States of America

08 07 06 05 04 03
8   7   6   5   4   3   2   1

Contents

1

WHY READ THE BIBLE?

Let's talk about the Bible. You're a new believer. You've accepted Jesus as your Savior. Now you need some practical guidance that will help you live this new life. You need to read the Bible.

Perhaps you've had one in your hands. You flipped it open, scanned some of the books, got really confused (perhaps you couldn't even understand some of the words, let alone the context), and put it aside as hopeless.

Maybe you've read a little bit. You began in Genesis and found it to be fairly interesting. Exodus was really good until about halfway through and then you began to get a little stuck. But you persevered—that is, until you hit Leviticus and all bets were off.

So what's in this book called the Bible? Other Christians you know claim it's the most important book in their lives. If they're called upon to open to a certain book of the Bible—they can do it! They seem to comprehend what's going on.

Well, fear not. You can do the same. And this little book will help you along the way.

God's Gift to You

I can still remember the first time I started to read this incredible book, the Bible. I was able to find a very understandable translation and that made a big difference. I soon discovered that this "user's manual" was the guide to life I had long been searching for. And it's available for you as well.

Although the Bible continues to be the best-selling book of all time, it's also true that very few people actually sit down and read it. Even among Christians there is sometimes a disconnect. Many crack open their Bibles only on Sunday mornings at church, whereas the rest of the week it gathers dust on the nightstand.

Some people may avoid reading the Bible because they just don't know what to do with it. It doesn't make sense. It's unlike any other book they've read. It's divided up funny. It has weird language. It seems almost archaic at times.

And yet it's very current. There's a single plot line and a central cast of characters. And what's really amazing is that it actually foretells the future.

But more about that later. First, to the issue at hand.

A *USA Today* survey of Americans revealed that more than 80 percent—including 71 percent of college graduates—believe the Bible is the inspired Word of God. Thirty-four percent believe the Bible is the actual Word of God, to be taken literally, word for word. However, the survey also revealed that people's beliefs *about* the Bible did not necessarily correspond to their familiarity with what the Bible actually says. For example, half of those who said they read the Bible regularly could not name any of the four Gospels of the New Testament. (The other 50 percent were able to name at least one.) Fewer than half knew who delivered the Sermon on the Mount. And even though 60 percent of Americans attend church on Easter Sunday, one-fourth did not know what the occasion signifies! That's definitely a problem.

So we have the Bible at our fingertips, but many of us don't read it! Meanwhile, there are people all over the world who would give anything to have a copy of the Bible to read for themselves. In some countries, a church might have a single Bible—which they cut apart in order to pass the pages around to the people in the congregation. A person might receive a page to read for a while and then pass it along to someone else in time to get the next page.

A typical Christian bookstore in the United States has an overwhelming array of Bibles for sale. There are countless versions, with various types of study aids and other tools, and several different translations—not to mention the variety of bindings, from hardback to paperback to genuine or bonded leather. Throw in all the different sizes and it can be mind-boggling!

Don't get me wrong. I think it's wonderful that we

have so many choices. What's sad is to have such an abundance and yet squander it. We have so much available, yet so few people read and treasure God's Word.

I'm reminded of a true story I heard about a young man graduating from college. He hoped that his dad would give him a new car for a graduation present. Many of the other kids' fathers had given them new cars, and this boy wanted one too. He had even picked out the one he wanted and told his father about it.

When graduation day finally arrived, the young man was shocked when his father handed him a brand new Bible instead of car keys. He was so outraged that he turned and walked away—leaving his father holding the Bible. The boy was so bitter that he cut off all contact with his father until the day his dad died.

Preparing for the funeral, the boy (now a man) went to his father's house to help get his affairs in order. There, sitting on a shelf, was the Bible his father had given him for graduation. With tears in his eyes, he blew off the dust and opened it for the first time. Much to his amazement, he found an envelope with his name on it tucked inside the Bible. He opened it and found a cashier's check in the exact amount of the car he had picked out years ago. In other words, his father *had* given him what he wanted, but he had to open the Bible to find out. Instead, he lost out on the car and a lifelong relationship with his father because he refused to open his Bible and discover the gift.

Sadly, that is essentially what we do when we never open the book that our heavenly Father has given us. Because inside this book is something far more valuable than a cashier's check.

The User's Manual for Life

In the Bible we find words of life. In it is the truth about how to get to heaven. In it are the very words of God to us. What could be more valuable than that?

Like any good instruction book, this "user's manual for life" tells us how to put it all together so that it works right. But if you're like me with most user's manuals, you're more likely to try out the gadget first and read the directions later (and usually end up doing something the manual says you *shouldn't* do).

Some products come with a warning label. Some of these labels are helpful, and some are just plain silly. But most labels are probably there because somebody, somewhere, did something they shouldn't have done. Here are a few examples of warning labels I have read:

- On a cardboard windshield shade: "Warning. Do not drive with sun shield in place."
- On a hair dryer: "Do not use while sleeping."
- On an electric rotary tool: "This product is not intended for use as a dental drill."

- In the manual for a microwave oven: "Do not use for drying pets."
- On a child-size Superman costume: "Wearing of this garment does not enable you to fly."

Think of those poor people who tried to dry their hair while sleeping or tried to fly because they had on a cape. If only they had read the directions and warnings first! The same is true of life. The Bible gives us directions and warnings because God knows how sinful we are.

The Bible has been used as a decoration on coffee tables, a booster seat for toddlers, a prop for preachers to wave in the air during a sermon, a place for witnesses to rest their left hand while taking an oath, or a convenient location to record the family tree.

But how often is the Bible *read*—and, most importantly, *obeyed?* Unfortunately, not often enough, even by Christians.

Don't make the same mistake.

The Bible is not a Christian prop; it's God's direct message to you. Why read the Bible? Here are four good reasons:

1. *Studying the Bible is necessary for your spiritual growth.* The Bible tells you everything you need to know to grow in your new spiritual life.
2. *Studying the Bible keeps you spiritually strong.* The more you get into this book and apply its

teachings, the more you will be able to stand
your ground in the storms and trials of life.
3. *Studying the Bible gives you a "biblical
   worldview."* During these confused times of
   moral relativism, God desires that you make
   the Bible an integral part of your life.
4. *Studying the Bible helps you apply its truth to
   your life.* You will notice positive changes in
   your life as you apply what you read in Scripture.

Listen! Success or failure in your Christian life depends on how much of the Bible you get into your
heart and mind on a daily basis and how obedient you
are to it. If you neglect to study the Scriptures, your
spiritual life will ultimately unravel. Everything you
need to know about God is taught in the Bible.

A Book unlike All Others
The Bible is altogether different from any other book
you'll ever read. Take your favorite novel, for example. After you've read it once or twice, you're done.
You might pick it up again a few years later just to re-
fresh your memory about a familiar story or a style of
writing that captured your imagination. But chances
are you read it once and moved on to something else.
The Bible, on the other hand, is not a book you'll
read through one time and return to the shelf to collect dust. The Bible is not a book that can be grasped

completely in one reading. Why? Because the Bible is a living book.

> *The word of God is living and active. Sharper than any double-edged sword, it penetrates even to dividing soul and spirit, joints and marrow; it judges the thoughts and attitudes of the heart.*
> *(Hebrews 4:12, NIV)*

You can read the same Bible passage a hundred times in your lifetime, and the one-hundred-first time you may discover something you never noticed before, or you may learn a lesson that applies to your life right at that moment.

> The Word of God is not simply a collection of words from God, a vehicle for communicating ideas; it is living, life-changing, and dynamic as it works in us. With the incisiveness of a surgeon's knife, God's Word reveals who we are and what we are not. It penetrates the core of our moral and spiritual life. It discerns what is within us, both good and evil. The demands of God's Word require decisions. We must not only listen to the Word; we must also let it shape our lives.[1]

That's why you want to keep reading it.
Yet there's more to it than just reading along to

---

[1] *Life Application Bible,* New International Version (Tyndale House and Zondervan, 1992), note on Hebrews 4:12.

feel good. You need to *study* the Bible in order to deepen your understanding and apply God's Word correctly. To make the most of your Bible study, you can read on your own and you can learn from others—pastors and teachers whose job it is to explain the Scriptures to you. You need to read the entire book so you can understand specific passages in their full context and so you can understand the entire scope of God's revealed will in a particular area. You need to understand the relationship of the Old Testament to the New Testament. In short, you need to become a *disciple*.

What It Means to Be a Disciple

The word *disciple* means "learner, a pupil, one who comes to be taught." However, the relationship is not merely that of a student listening passively to a lecturer. A disciple listens attentively, with an intense desire to apply what is being taught, drinking in every word, marking every vocal inflection. We need inspired preaching and teaching, but we also need inspired *listening!*

Think of a pitcher and catcher in a baseball game. The catcher doesn't sit idly behind the plate, waiting for the pitch to hit his glove at speeds approaching one hundred miles per hour. If he did, he might get his head knocked off! Instead, he carefully watches each pitch and positions his glove and his body accordingly. The catcher is just as much a part of the game as the pitcher. The two are working together toward a common goal: striking out the batter.

As you sit in the pew on Sunday morning, the Holy Spirit is like the pitcher and you are like the catcher. The more attentive you are in listening to the Word of God, the greater the chances that each "pitch" will be a strike. You and the Holy Spirit share a common goal: that you will grow and flourish spiritually. It's all about learning how to listen!

This is why Jesus so often said, "Anyone who is willing to hear should listen and understand!" (Matthew 11:15; 13:9; 13:43).

Sometimes we listen more carefully than at other times. For example, how many times have you tuned out aboard an airplane while the flight attendant explained what to do in case of an emergency landing? How different would it be if you were flying across the Atlantic Ocean and the flight attendant announced that the plane was having engine trouble? All of a sudden, you'd be very interested in knowing that your seat cushion could be used as a flotation device. Why? Because your life would depend on it!

In the same way, your spiritual life depends on studying God's Word. Simply listening to what Jesus teaches does not make anyone a true disciple. Only those who listen and *obey* what He says will be saved from destruction. If you and I want to be true disciples of Jesus Christ, we must study the Word and apply what we read. As the apostle Paul said, "Do not be conformed to this world, but be transformed by the renewing of your mind, that you may prove what the will of God is, that which is good and acceptable and perfect" (Romans 12:2, NASB).

Here is a wonderful series of promises that will help us get the most from our study of Scripture:

> *My child, listen to me and treasure my instructions. Tune your ears to wisdom, and concentrate on understanding. Cry out for insight and understanding. Search for them as you would for lost money or hidden treasure. Then you will understand what it means to fear the Lord, and you will gain knowledge of God. For the Lord grants wisdom! From his mouth come knowledge and understanding. He grants a treasure of good sense to the godly. He is their shield, protecting those who walk with integrity. He guards the paths of justice and protects those who are faithful to him. Then you will understand what is right, just, and fair, and you will know how to find the right course of action every time. (Proverbs 2:1-9)*

Let's take a closer look at three key principles from this passage in Proverbs:

Listen to God and Treasure His Instructions
First, you must see the intrinsic value of God's Word. This means you should be eager with anticipation

when you open the Bible, asking, "What will God say to me today?" As you read, it's important to stop and think about what God might be showing you. Some people like to keep a journal where they can record thoughts, questions, prayers, and insights. This can be a helpful tool in your study.

Take your time and meditate on what you read. You don't need to read entire chapters or books at a time. Sometimes a few verses or paragraphs are all one can absorb. As you read, ask God to teach you how to treasure His Word.

Cry Out for Insight and Understanding

God doesn't expect you to understand everything you read right away. He knows this is all new to you. He lovingly offers to guide and teach you. His Holy Spirit will give you insight and understanding. Tell God you need His help. Cry out to Him for the insight and understanding you need to be able to learn and apply His words to your life.

Seek Wisdom As If You Were Searching for Lost Money or Hidden Treasure

Want to attract a crowd? Drop a handful of change! Likewise, if you want to know God, He tells you to seek Him and His wisdom as though you were looking for lost money or digging for hidden treasure.

Listen! There is buried treasure in the Bible! But you can only find it when you search.

Help for Daily Living

Proverbs 2:9 records an outstanding promise. Read it again:

> *You will understand what is right, just, and fair, and you will know how to find the right course of action every time.*

When you've listened to God and treasured His instructions, cried out for understanding, and sought His will in His word as if looking for treasure—*guess what?* You'll find the answers you need. You'll understand the right, just, and fair thing to do, and you'll know the right course of action every time!

Jesus says, "If you continue in my word, you are truly my disciples" (John 8:31, NRSV). The word *continue* here is the same word he uses in John 15:7 where He speaks of "remaining" or "abiding" in His word: "If you abide in me, and my words abide in you, ask for whatever you wish, and it will be done for you" (John 15:7, NRSV). The word *abide* means to stay in a given place, to draw strength and resources from God. Picture a tree firmly planted in the ground. So we are to be planted in the Word.

Psalm 1 says that we should meditate on God's Word "day and night" (Psalm 1:2, NIV). If we are abiding in the Word, it means we're drawing our ideas and lifestyle from the Word, and what we say and do will be affected.

Abiding in God's Word can transform your life. It

will sustain you through the difficulties you face each day. It will help you with your thought life. It will guide you as you conduct yourself at school, at home, and even in your free time. It will help you make decisions. It will comfort you. It will challenge you. It will change you from the inside out.

It is only when you put yourself under the authority of God's Word and submit to its teaching that you become a growing disciple. Colossians 3:16 says, "Let the word of Christ dwell in you richly" (NRSV). This literally means to "let the Word of Christ be perfectly at home in you." God wants his Word to permeate every area of your life.

2

WHAT THE BIBLE SAYS ABOUT ITSELF

In the Bible, you will find a variety of words used to describe God's Word:

- command (or commands)
- commandments
- decrees
- law (or laws)
- precepts
- word (or words) of God

Don't be intimidated. Although a collection of laws, commands, and decrees might sound kind of dry to some, you'll soon discover that these precepts and principles often appear as part of exciting stories about people who obey or disobey God, in passionate speeches, or through amazing revelations. You'll also discover that these commandments are not dry at all, but like water to your thirsty soul or honey to your sweet tooth. For example, consider these verses from one of the beautiful songs found in the middle of your Bible in the collection called the Psalms:

> The law of the Lord is perfect,
>   reviving the soul.
> The decrees of the Lord are trustworthy,
>   making wise the simple.
> The commandments of the Lord are right,
>   bringing joy to the heart.
> The commands of the Lord are clear,
>   giving insight to life.
> Reverence for the Lord is pure,
>   lasting forever.
> The laws of the Lord are true;
>   each one is fair.
> They are more desirable than gold,
>   even the finest gold.
> They are sweeter than honey,
>   even honey dripping from the comb.
> They are a warning to those who hear them;
>   there is great reward for those who obey
>   them. (Psalm 19:7-11)

The Word of God Is Perfect

This phrase "the law of the Lord" is a Hebrew term used to define the Scriptures. We are told "the law of the Lord is *perfect*." In other words, there is nothing to be added or taken away from it. The Bible says, "All Scripture is inspired by God and is useful to teach us what is true and to make us realize what is wrong in our lives. It straightens us out and teaches us to do what is right. It is God's way of preparing us in every way, fully equipped for every good thing God wants us to do" (2 Timothy 3:16-17).

The assertion that "all Scripture is inspired by God" literally means "all Scripture is God-*breathed*." In other words, the Bible is God's infallible Word. The first copies of the Scriptures (sometimes called by scholars the "original autographs") were without error. There are no mistakes, no contradictions; it is perfect. Some recent discoveries, such as the Dead Sea Scrolls, have shown that the Bible we read today is still basically the same as what was written thousands of years ago!

The Bible is the only book you need to discover the foundational truths of how to know God and walk with Him. The Bible is your source for truth. As our society continues to change (almost always for the worse), you don't need to be blown about by the winds of change. You can stand on the firm foundation of God's Word. You can know what's right and what's wrong. Remember, the Bible is indeed the user's manual for life—a *perfect* manual with no mistakes.

The Word of God Transforms

"The law of the Lord is perfect, *reviving the soul*" (Psalm 19:7, emphasis added). Someone who says, "I'm not really interested in changing or being transformed" is probably not interested in the Bible. The truths found in the Bible will change your life. "For the word of God is full of living power. It is sharper than the sharpest knife, cutting deep into our inner-most thoughts and desires. It exposes us for what we really are" (Hebrews 4:12). If you have a sense of desperation about the circumstances of your life, you will find hope and peace. If you lack purpose in your life, you will discover that God created you for a purpose and that your life has meaning. If you're not sure where you came from or where you're going, you will find direction and guidance. If you have things in your life that you wish you could change, you will find that God has the power to make all things brand-new:

- No longer do you need to be controlled by your passions.
- No longer will you be a mere victim of your circumstances.
- No longer must you cope alone with the pain in your life.
- No longer must you only wish that your relationships with others were better.

The Bible was written for people who don't have all the answers and who want something better. Even when you don't understand everything you read, even when you can't see the changes occurring in your life, it doesn't thwart God's purpose. Like a plant drawing minerals from the soil where it is planted, you are absorbing minerals of truth from the soil of God's Word. The prophet Isaiah writes:

> *The rain and snow come down from the heavens
> and stay on the ground to water the earth. They
> cause the grain to grow, producing seed for the
> farmer and bread for the hungry. It is the same
> with my word. I send it out, and it always pro-
> duces fruit. It will accomplish all I want it to,
> and it will prosper everywhere I send it. (Isaiah
> 55:10-11)*

If you're struggling with your attempts to read the Bible, don't be discouraged. Maybe you don't know exactly what's going on or why something is happening
or who the prophet Isaiah is, but keep reading. God
promises that His Word "always produces fruit." You
may not understand all about minerals and how they
go from the soil to the plant—all you know is that a
plant dies if it isn't rooted in the ground. Take up
those minerals and let God provide the growth in
you. As you keep reading, attending church, and
learning, pretty soon the pieces will begin to come together and make more and more sense. And God will
keep his Word working in your life—even when you
don't understand it all. Slowly but surely it will work a
transformation in your life. Watch and see!

The Word of God Gives Wisdom

"The decrees of the Lord are trustworthy, *making wise
the simple*" (Psalm 19:7, emphasis added). The Hebrew word translated *simple* comes from a root that

speaks of an open door. The "simple" person, then, has a mind like an open door—everything comes in and goes out. This person does not know what to keep in or keep out. He is totally naive, open to everything, closed to nothing. The Bible says it is able to make such a person wise!

I was not raised in a Christian home. When I was in my teens and asked the Lord to come into my life, I began to read the Bible for the first time. I was amazed at how completely relevant it was to my life. At times I was surprised to find the ink was dry on its pages because it seemed as if it had been written just for me only moments before:

- When I needed to know about relationships, I found a lot of examples in the Bible—good examples, bad examples, and wise counsel about how to be a good friend, spouse, boss, and employee.
- When I needed to know about marriage, I discovered that the Bible has a lot to say about that, too.
- When I wanted to know how to live life to its fullest, I found that the Bible answered my questions.
- When I wanted to learn how to be wise, I knew I'd come to the right place.

How can one book do all that? Remember Isaiah's prophecy quoted above: God will make His Word produce fruit in your life. Sometimes one verse will stand out to you and give you direction in a particular situation. Sometimes the story of a person's struggles will give you insight into how to (or how not to) act in your own life. You gain wisdom because you're following God's directions. You're learning how to become wise.

The Word of God Is Right

"The commandments of the Lord are *right*" (Psalm 19:8, emphasis added). In Hebrew, this declaration means that the Bible has set out the right path for you to follow. The Bible teaches you right and wrong in your life. Take another look at 2 Timothy 3:16-17: "All Scripture is inspired by God and is useful to teach us what is true and to make us realize what is wrong in our lives. It straightens us out and teaches us to do what is right. It is God's way of preparing us in every way, fully equipped for every good thing God wants us to do."

This is why it is essential to read the Word of God. Consider this promise to those who will do what the Lord wants:

> Oh, the joys of those
>> who do not follow the advice of the wicked,
>> or stand around with sinners,
>> or join in with scoffers.
> But they delight in doing everything the LORD
>> wants;

> *day and night they think about his law.*
> *They are like trees planted along the riverbank,*
>   *bearing fruit each season without fail.*
> *Their leaves never wither,*
>   *and in all they do, they prosper.*
> *But this is not true of the wicked.*
>   *They are like worthless chaff, scattered by the*
>   *wind.*
> *They will be condemned at the time of*
>   *judgment.*
>   *Sinners will have no place among the godly.*
> *For the Lord watches over the path of the godly,*
>   *but the path of the wicked leads to*
>   *destruction. (Psalm 1:1-6)*

Psalm 119:9 says, "How can a young person stay pure? By obeying your word and following its rules." The apostle Paul writes to his young friend Timothy: "Work hard so God can approve you. Be a good worker, one who does not need to be ashamed and who correctly explains the word of truth" (2 Timothy 2:15).

To know God, you must first know His Word.

I heard the story of an old recluse who lived deep in the mountains of Colorado. When he died, some of his distant relatives came from the city to collect his valuables. Upon arriving, all they found was an old shack with an outhouse beside it. Inside the shack, next to the rock fireplace, was an old cooking pot and some mining equipment. A cracked table with a three-legged chair stood guard by a tiny window, and an old kerosene lamp served as the centerpiece for the table. In the dark corner of the little room was a dilapidated cot with a bedroll on it. Deciding there was nothing there of value, the family members left.

As they were driving away, an old friend of the recluse flagged them down. "Y'all mind if I help myself to what's left in my friend's cabin?" he asked.

"Go right ahead," they replied. After all, they thought, nothing inside the shack was worth anything.

The old friend entered the shack and walked directly over to the table. He reached underneath and lifted up one of the floorboards, then proceeded to take out all the gold his friend had discovered in the past fifty-three years—*it was worth millions!* Apparently the recluse had died with only his close friend knowing his true worth. As the friend looked out the little window and watched the disappearing cloud of dust behind the family members' car, he said, "They shoulda got to know him better!"

The same is true with us and our friend Jesus Christ. So many Christians behave like distant relatives, even though Jesus has invited us to intimate friendship.

Jesus has many wonderful treasures to reveal to you from His Word. Those treasures will set you on the pathway to a completely fulfilling life, for you will be doing exactly what God has prepared for you to do. His Word is right, and it shows the right way for you to go.

The Word of God Brings Happiness

The Word of God brings "joy to the heart" (Psalm 19:8). If you want peace, joy, meaning, and purpose in life, you've come to the right place. Jesus said, "Blessed . . . are those who hear the word of God and obey it" (Luke 11:28, NIV).

Perhaps you're looking at your Bible, with all its small print and confusing words, and the prospect of reading it doesn't make you very happy or joyful.

Trust me. Dig in. Search for the treasure. Let God make it work in your life. You'll discover that the Bible is indeed "more desirable than gold" and "sweeter than honey, even honey dripping from the comb."

God gives you a promise. Not only does He set His Word to work in your life, but He adds that "there is great reward for those who obey" His Word. Jesus said to the Jews who believed Him, "You are truly my disciples if you keep obeying my teachings. And you will know the truth, and the truth will set you free" (John 8:31-32). Now that's happiness!

3

HOW YOU CAN KNOW
THE BIBLE IS TRUE

You may be saying to yourself, "That's all well and good what the Bible says about itself. But I can say a lot of things about myself, too, and that doesn't make them *true!*"

That's a fair statement. After all, if you're going to stake your life on something, you need to know it's worth that kind of commitment.

Let's talk about how you can know that the Bible is true. I am indebted to my friend John MacArthur for the following outline on the truthfulness of Scripture.

I know the Bible is true because it is confirmed by my experience.

Personal experience is not the only reason I believe in the truth of Scripture, and it's perhaps not the most convincing evidence to skeptics, but it has certainly helped me to believe. For example, the Bible says that God will forgive my sins:

> *If we confess our sins to him, he is faithful and just
> to forgive us and to cleanse us from every wrong.
> (1 John 1:9)*

One day I chose to believe that. I accepted God's
forgiveness—and you know what? The sense of guilt
and the heavy burden I had been carrying was taken
away.

The Bible also says that if I come to Jesus, I will become a different person:

> *Those who become Christians become new per-
> sons. They are not the same anymore, for the old
> life is gone. A new life has begun! (2 Corinthians
> 5:17)*

I trusted my life to Jesus and I've been transformed. I'm still a "work in progress," of course, but
the change has happened.

The Bible says that God will give me His peace and
joy if I trust Christ:

> *I am leaving you with a gift—peace of mind and
> heart. And the peace I give isn't like the peace the
> world gives. So don't be troubled or afraid. . . .
> You haven't done this before. Ask, using my
> name, and you will receive, and you will have
> abundant joy. (John 14:27; 16:24)*

Since I became a Christian, I have experienced

times of wonderful peace and incredible joy—just as He promised.

The Bible says that God will answer my prayers (if I pray properly):

If you believe, you will receive whatever you ask for in prayer. (Matthew 21:22)

I believe what the Bible says, and my prayers have been answered.

If you read the Bible, you will discover it is full of promises made to God's people—which now includes you. As you live your new Christian life, you will find the truth of God's Word borne out in your daily experience.

I know the Bible is true because it is confirmed by science.

You might be thinking, "No, the Bible and science contradict each other." That is not necessarily true. There are many who have scoffed at the Bible, saying how unscientific it is. Yet it was the Bible that first said that the number of the stars is beyond counting. Scripture says that God "stretched forth the heavens" (Isaiah 51:13, KJV) into a limitless expanse which can never be measured and filled it with "countless millions" of stars (Genesis 22:17). To the average observer looking into the sky with the latest telescope technology, the visible stars are not uncountable.

There are a vast number, but they do not seem impossible to count. Yet the Bible flatly states that the number of the stars can be compared, literally, to the number of the grains of sand upon the seashore. Modern science has now established this to be true. People cannot possibly begin to assess the number of the stars.

The Bible also says that God "suspends the earth over nothing" (Job 26:7, NIV). In that poetic way it describes the mysterious force of gravity, which no one even yet understands but which keeps the earth suspended in its relationship to the sun and the other planets. As the Bible says, the earth literally hangs upon nothing.

The Bible says, "Things which are seen were not made of things which do appear" (Hebrews 11:3, KJV), thus predating by many centuries the discoveries of modern science that finally recognized that all matter is made up of invisible energy and that matter and energy are interchangeable.

I don't believe in the Bible because science proves that it's true; rather, I believe in the science that the Bible proves is true.

Having said all that, let me point out something that is very important for us to know about the Bible. It is not the Bible's purpose to be a textbook on science. If it were, the book would be much thicker than it is and probably much less comprehensible. Rather, the Bible is intended to be a book of *redemption*. Its primary purpose is not to tell us *how the heavens go,* but *how to go to heaven.* It tells us how to know God and how to live as part of this troubled and confused human race. It is the only book that speaks with authority in this realm.

I know the Bible is true because it is confirmed by archaeology.

Over the years, countless critics have challenged the teachings of the Bible. But recent archaeological findings have confirmed Scripture's teachings time and time again.

For years, many skeptics doubted that crucifixion took place at all. Contrary to Scripture, they contended that Christ's crucifixion never happened. You can see how such criticism strikes at the very heart of our faith. But these contrary voices were silenced in 1968 when the remains of a crucified man were discovered north of Jerusalem. The skeleton had a seven-inch iron nail still embedded in the heel, and the state of the bones indicated that his arms had been outstretched. Once again, the Bible gave the information before the "experts" had it.

Others doubted the Bible because they could find no historical record of a Roman governor named Pontius Pilate. But in 1961 an inscription found at Caesarea Maritima confirmed that Pontius Pilate was the Roman governor in Judea at the time of Jesus' crucifixion.

Some doubted Scripture's authority because no record of a high priest named Caiaphas existed. But in 1990, Caiaphas's tomb was discovered.

Now there is a possibility that archaeologists have found Noah's ark. On September 25, 2000, *U.S. News & World Report* published a story about some archaeologists, led by oceanographer Robert Ballard (who found the Titanic), who have been searching beneath the Black Sea off the Turkish coast for evidence of an apocalyptic natural event that could have inspired the Genesis account of the great flood. The expedition found a large wooden building twelve miles offshore at a depth of more than three hundred feet. The explorers also found ample evidence of a widespread flood, just as the Bible says. Could this wooden structure be Noah's ark? I don't know, but in any case, I don't believe the Bible is true because archaeology confirms it. I believe archaeology is true because the Bible confirms it.

I know the Bible is true because it is confirmed by its many prophecies that have come true.

When we talk about Bible prophecies, we don't mean tabloid predictions; we're referring to very specific prophecies that have been fulfilled over a span of hundreds of years. No other religion has prophets who predict the future with such uncanny accuracy as the prophets in the Bible.

Why not? If they were to attempt it, it would soon

be evident that they are not inspired by God. God can speak of the future with absolute certainty because He knows it as well as we know the past.

The basic test of true prophets—and by extension the one true God and the one true faith—is this: Can they predict the future without error? The Bible is full of stories about prophets who predicted future events, not just once or twice, but *hundreds of times!* And many more prophecies have yet to be fulfilled—but they will be.

It is worth noting that two-thirds of the Bible consists of prophecy. One-half of these prophecies have already been fulfilled. If half of the prophecies have already come true just as the Bible said, should I have any reason to doubt that the remaining ones will happen exactly as God has promised? When God says something is going to happen, you can take it to the bank.

A college professor asked his class to estimate the odds of having eight prophecies fulfilled by one man:

- The odds that he would be born in Bethlehem (predicted in Micah 5:2, fulfilled in Matthew 2:1): 1 in 280,000
- The odds that a forerunner would announce his coming (predicted in Malachi 3:1, fulfilled in Luke 3:4): 1 in 1,000
- The odds that he would ride into Jerusalem on a donkey (predicted in Zechariah 9:9, fulfilled in Matthew 21:1-10): 1 in 1,000

- The odds that he would be betrayed by a friend and his hands and feet would be pierced (predicted in Psalm 22:16; Zechariah 13:6, fulfilled in Luke 23:33): 1 in 1,000
- The odds that he would be betrayed for thirty pieces of silver (predicted in Zechariah 11:12, fulfilled in Matthew 26:14-16): 1 in 10,000
- The odds that the one who betrayed him would throw the thirty pieces of silver down in the temple and that the money would be used to purchase a potter's field (predicted in Zechariah 11:13, fulfilled in Matthew 27:5-7): 1 in 100,000
- The odds that he would offer no defense when placed on trial for his life (predicted in Isaiah 53:7, fulfilled in Mathew 26:62-63; Mark 14:60-61): 1 in 10,000
- The odds that he would be executed by crucifixion (predicted in Psalm 22:16, fulfilled in Luke 23:32-33): 1 in 10,000

If you put all these together and divide by the total number of people who have lived since the time of these prophecies, the odds that all eight prophecies would be fulfilled by one person, Jesus Christ, is 1:10. (That's a one followed by twenty-one zeroes!) Here's another way to look at it: If you were to cover the entire land mass of the earth with silver dollars 120 feet deep, mark one of the coins, and then blindfold someone and ask him to walk around the world and randomly reach down and pick the one that was marked, he would have as much of a chance of choosing the right coin as Jesus had of fulfilling those eight prophecies. And yet, Jesus not only fulfilled the eight prophecies I mentioned, he also fulfilled many others.[2]

Despite this compelling evidence, the accuracy of the Bible—and the truth about Jesus—is continually under attack in our society.

There will always be critics who want to point their finger at the Bible and question its authenticity. There will be groups who will try to cut it apart, saying this part is true and that part isn't. Ultimately, the issue of believing the Bible comes down to faith.

As you establish a habit of reading your Bible, you will discover that you won't be able to explain everything you read. That's okay. You see, the Bible is not meant to be a scientific textbook. Instead, it is the story of salvation. It explains the basic problem with humanity (our sin), the trouble we get into as a result of sin, and God's solution to our problem—sending Jesus to die on our behalf, to pay the price for our sin, and to break its power in our lives.

Essentially, that's it. From Genesis to Revelation, the Bible is one long story with a common theme. Dr. W. A. Criswell, the late pastor of First Baptist Church in Dallas, used to call it "the scarlet thread of redemption."

---

[2]For a discussion of how these numbers were derived, see Peter W. Stoner, *Science Speaks* (Wheaton, Ill.: Van Kampen, 1952), 70–79.

Technically speaking, the Bible is not *one* book; it is actually sixty-six books written over a 1,500-year span. It was written by more than forty authors from every walk of life, including kings, peasants, philosophers, fishermen, poets, statesmen, and scholars. Writers include Moses, a political leader trained in the universities of Egypt; Peter, a fisherman; Joshua, a military general; Daniel, a prime minister; Luke, a doctor; Solomon, a king; Matthew, a tax collector; Paul, a rabbi.

The Bible was written in different places. Moses and David often wrote in the wilderness; Jeremiah, in a dungeon; Daniel, on a hillside and in a palace; Paul, inside prison walls; Luke, while traveling, often by ship.

Each one of these men was inspired by God to write their words. God used these different writers—with their personal perspectives and even the different audiences to whom they wrote—and inspired their writing so that it is, literally, *God's words.*

In spite of great diversity of authorship in the OT [Old Testament] and NT [New Testament], and composition spanning over 1,500 years, there is remarkable unity in the total thrust. Christians believe that God must have been superintending the production of a divine-human book that would properly present his message to humankind.

The OT and NT are component parts of one divine revelation. The OT describes man and woman in the first paradise on the old earth; the NT concludes with a vision of the new heaven and the new earth. The OT sees humankind as fallen from a sinless condition and separated from God; the NT views believers as restored to favor through the sacrifice of Christ. The OT predicts a coming Redeemer who will rescue men and women from eternal condemnation; the NT reveals the Christ who brought salvation. In most of the OT the spotlight focuses on a sacrificial system in which the blood of animals provided a temporary handling of the sin problem; in the New, Christ appeared as the one who came to put an end to all sacrifice—to be himself the supreme sacrifice. In the OT, numerous predictions foretold a coming Messiah who would save his people; in the New, scores of passages detail how those prophecies were minutely fulfilled in the person of Jesus Christ. . . . As Augustine said more than 1,500 years ago, "The New is in the Old contained; the Old is in the New explained."[3]

The following quote explains what Christians mean when we talk about the Bible being "inspired" by God.

[3]Walter A. Elwell and Philip W. Comfort, eds., *Tyndale Bible Dictionary* (Wheaton, Ill.: 2001), 169.

The Bible is not a collection of stories, fables, myths, or merely human ideas about God. It is not a human book. Through the Holy Spirit, God revealed his person and plan to certain believers, who wrote down his message for his people (2 Peter 1:20-21). This process is known as inspiration. The writers wrote from their own personal, historical, and cultural contexts. Although they used their own minds, talents, language, and style, they wrote what God wanted them to write. Scripture is completely trustworthy because God was in control of its writing. Its words are entirely authoritative for our faith and lives. The Bible is "God-breathed." Read it, and use its teachings to guide your conduct.[4]

All these different people, across a span of centuries, wrote a book that ultimately tells one story: why people need to be saved and how God provided for salvation. The complexity and cohesiveness of the Bible couldn't "just happen." Only God, through His Holy Spirit, working through human writers, could have developed this incredible book—God's true and everlasting words to *you.*

---

[4]*Life Application Bible,* New International Version (Tyndale House and Zondervan, 1992), note on 2 Timothy 3:16.

4

HOW TO STUDY THE BIBLE

If I have convinced you that it's important to get into God's Word so that God's Word can get into you— great!

But now what?

Well, let's dig in.

Getting Started on Bible Study

Get a Bible

You may already have a Bible. However, if it is an older translation, you may find that the language in it is very difficult to read and understand. Fortunately, Christian translators have worked hard to continually update the Bible's language, making it very easy to read and easier to understand. So if you have a King James Version and you can't understand a thing it says—don't worry. Take a trip to your local Christian bookstore. You'll be amazed to discover the variety of translations and study Bibles that are now available. (For help in wading through your many options, see the section at the end of this chapter called Choosing a Bible.)

Set Aside Some Quiet Time

You've probably heard other Christians talk about having their "quiet time" or their "devotions." They are referring to their own private Bible reading and prayer time. All believers need to set aside time *every day* to read their Bibles and pray. Sadly, many Christians don't do this—to their own detriment. This is a time when you and God can talk. It's your opportunity to sit down with someone who loves you very much and who wants to guide you through the day ahead. Why would you miss that appointment?

Look at your schedule and set aside at least a few minutes every day to study God's Word and pray. There's no right or wrong way to do this—just find a time that works for you. Maybe you need to get up a bit earlier, when the house is quiet and you won't be interrupted. Maybe you can do it over lunch. Perhaps the best time for you will be right before you go to bed. The point is to schedule a time so that it becomes a habit to spend time with God.

This may be one of the biggest changes you'll see in your life—this scheduled time to read the Bible and pray. But it is this very important habit that will provide the foundation for your Christian life. As I've noted in previous chapters, you *need* God's Word, and the only way to get it is to spend time reading it every day.

Pray for Wisdom and Understanding

The most often overlooked and undervalued aspect of Bible study is prayer. Prayer is essential to gaining wisdom and understanding when you read God's Word. Through prayer, you can approach God and acknowledge your incomplete knowledge of His Word, as well as your need for Him to open your heart to His instruction. Therefore, determine to begin each study with prayer. Only God can give you the wisdom to understand His Word.

Here's a simple prayer you can pray:

> *Lord, I'm new to Bible study and prayer—yet I understand how important they are for me to grow spiritually. As I open your Word today, teach me something that will help me through my day.*

Read in an Orderly Manner

If you received a letter and read only a few sentences here and there, the letter would not make much sense to you. But if you read the letter from beginning to end, you would understand it. The same holds true when you read the Bible.

This is where a lot of people get off track in their study of the Bible. They adopt a "hunt and peck" method—a little bit from Genesis . . . throw in a few verses from Matthew . . . take a quick dash through Jude . . . and top it off with a heavy dose of Revelation. The result, as you might expect, is spiritual indigestion.

One danger of taking a haphazard approach to reading the Bible is that we might be tempted to isolate passages and take them out of context. (This is done regularly in many cult groups.) For instance, let's take a look at Philippians 2:12:

> *Therefore, my beloved, as you have always obeyed, not as in my presence only, but now much more in my absence, work out your own salvation with fear and trembling. (NKJV)*

Some have used this verse to say, "You have to *work* for your salvation." But if you read the following verse, Philippians 2:13, you gain some valuable perspective:

> *For it is God who works in you both to will and to do for His good pleasure. (NKJV)*

Context is very important in understanding and interpreting Scripture. It's also important to consider other verses that speak to the same subject. For example, Ephesians 2:8-9 gives us more information about whether we need to work for our salvation:

> *For it is by grace you have been saved, through faith—and this not from yourselves, it is the gift of God—not by works, so that no one can boast. (NIV)*

You can see why a thorough and systematic study of the Bible is so important if we want to understand

God's message to us. It doesn't necessarily mean that you have to read straight through from Genesis to Revelation. Work on one book at a time, but keep going until you have finished the entire Bible. It might be easier to begin in the New Testament, perhaps with the Gospel of John. This book was written to help us see that Jesus is the Son of God. After you have finished reading John, read the rest of the New Testament. Once you have finished the New Testament, which covers the life of Jesus on earth and the establishment of the early church, start reading the Old Testament, which tells the story of the nation of Israel and foreshadows the coming of Jesus the Messiah.

Make it your goal to read the whole Bible—but not before next Sunday. Take your time, and read thoroughly. At the end of this book is a reading plan to help you read through the entire New Testament in a year. There are other reading plans available that will help you read through the entire Bible in a year (for example, at a Christian bookstore you can purchase a one-year Bible that already has the text divided up by days of the year).

Every book in the Bible is included for a reason. Reading everything will help you become familiar with the "whole counsel of God."

Finish What You Start
In life, the benefits of doing anything are often not realized until the task is completed. The same is true of read-

ing a book from the Bible. Once you've chosen a book to read, read it from beginning to end. Although you may benefit spiritually by reading a verse from one book or a story from another, you will profit more by reading the entire book because it puts each verse and story in its proper context. Thus, you will have a better understanding of what it means. In addition, by reading books from beginning to end, you will become more familiar with the Bible as a whole. You may even discover passages that will one day become your favorites.

Meditate on God's Word and Ask Questions

I cannot overemphasize the importance of taking time to think about what you have read. As you meditate on God's Word, He will help you discover the importance of each passage of Scripture. It will also help you examine your life in light of what God has revealed in His Word.

When I use the word *meditate,* I'm not referring to transcendental meditation or the New Age practice of emptying your mind. The biblical idea of meditation means to "chew something over," to contemplate or consider. One of the best ways to begin meditating on God's Word is to ask questions. Here are a few questions to help you get started:

- What is the main subject of the passage?
- To whom is the passage addressed?
- Who is speaking?
- About what or whom is the person speaking?

Take a couple of minutes to think about each passage you read. If you read a whole chapter, you might need to break it down into paragraphs to help you in your understanding. Then, for each section, ask these two questions:

- What is the key verse?
- What does this passage teach me about God?

Next, to see how the text might apply to you personally, ask yourself these questions:

- Is there any *sin* mentioned in the passage that I need to confess or forsake?
- Is there a *command* given that I should obey?
- Is there a *promise* made that I can apply to my current circumstances?
- Is there a *prayer* given that I could pray?

Invest in a Few Good Resource Books

The Bible alludes to many ancient customs that are completely unfamiliar to us today. Much of the subtle meaning behind these allusions that would give us greater insight into and appreciation for God's Word is therefore lost. To understand the culture in which the Bible was written, you may want to purchase a few good biblical resource books.

There are two types of books you should consider purchasing: a one- or two-volume commentary on the whole Bible, and a Bible dictionary. Most one- or two-volume commentaries are concise. They give you the necessary information on important words, phrases, and verses from the Bible. They will not comment on every verse, and they will not give a detailed explanation of any one verse, but they are good resources to help you begin to understand God's Word.

Bible dictionaries contain short articles (in alphabetical order) on people, places, and objects found in the Bible. Some Bible dictionaries also contain maps, diagrams, and pictures of cities, regions, and artifacts.

Here's a short list of resources that you may find helpful in your study of the Bible:

- *Life Application New Testament Commentary* (Tyndale House Publishers)
- *Halley's Bible Handbook*
- The "Be" series of commentaries by Warren Wiersbe
- *New Believer's Bible* (Tyndale House Publishers)
- *Tyndale Bible Dictionary* (Tyndale House Publishers)
- I have done extensive teaching on Old and New Testament books, and these messages are available on CD and audio cassette. For more information, log on to www.harvest.org.

Choosing a Bible
What about All These Bible Translations?
If you're in the market for a Bible, you might find

yourself confused by the huge variety available. Various publishers have done lots of hard work to help make the Bible understandable and helpful. In this section, I've listed some of the most common Bible versions you will find at most Christian bookstores. I've also included a brief overview of each version (from the *Essential Guide to Bible Versions* by Philip W. Comfort).

The original texts of the Bible were written in Hebrew (Old Testament) and Greek (New Testament). Later some Jewish scholars translated the Hebrew Old Testament into Greek because Greek was the everyday language of much of the world, beginning about two hundred years before the time of Christ. Eventually the entire text of the Bible was translated into Latin.

Unfortunately, as the influence of the Roman Empire waned, soon only priests and scholars, who had been trained in the classical languages, could read the Latin Scriptures. In Great Britain, William Tyndale (1484–1536), who is known as "The Father of the English Bible," wanted to translate the Bible into English so the common people could read it. However, he could not get permission from the government, so he went to Germany and was able to publish an English translation of the New Testament in 1526. By 1530, he had completed the first five books of the Old Testament (Genesis, Exodus, Leviticus, Numbers, and Deuteronomy—also called the Pentateuch).

However, he was later found guilty of heresy because of his translation work and was burned at the stake in 1536. Since then, the Bible has been translated into hundreds of languages, and dozens of English translations are available. Here's a brief overview of the major translations currently available:

King James Version (KJV), New King James Version (NKJV)

William Tyndale's work formed the foundation for what would eventually be the most significant English Bible translation ever completed—what came to be called the King James Version, published in 1611. This version was prepared at the request of King James I of England and became the standard English version of the Bible for three centuries. In fact, you can still purchase the King James Version. Many people still prefer it for the eloquence of its language. I was raised studying the King James Version and still love and value it.

The KJV includes archaic pronouns like "thee" and "thou" and may be a bit difficult to read. However, you can also find a version called the New King James Version, published in 1982, which replaces much of the archaic language with more current terms.

Revised Standard Version (RSV), New Revised Standard Version (NRSV)

These translations are exactly what the name suggests: revisions of earlier texts. As language evolves, many Bible translations are updated accordingly. In

1952, the American Standard Version, an earlier translation of the Bible, was updated and revised. The result was the Revised Standard Version. Today you will also find the New Revised Standard Version, which was published in 1990 to update the RSV.

New American Standard Bible (NASB)

The NASB is another revision of the American Standard Version, this one published by the Lockman Foundation in 1971. The translators of this version attempted to adhere to the style and syntax of the original languages while creating an easily readable English version.

New International Version (NIV)

The New International Version is a completely new rendering of the original languages done by a group of international scholars (hence the "international" in the title). They worked to provide a thought-for-thought translation in contemporary English. They were working to find a point midway between a literal rendering (such as in the NASB) and a more free-flowing translation. They wanted to pass along, in readable English, the thoughts of the original writers. The complete NIV was first published in 1978, was revised and updated in 1984, and is still in wide use today.

New Century Version (NCV)

Another translation from the original languages is available in an edition called *The Everyday Bible*. First published in 1993, the NCV emphasizes simplicity and clarity. It was meant to be easy even for children to read, so the translators used short sentences and third-grade level vocabulary.

Contemporary English Version (CEV)

The CEV takes technical terms such as "salvation," "grace," and "righteousness" (words that may not be clearly understood by many readers) and changes them to natural English equivalents such as "God saves you," "God is kind to you," and "God accepts you." This contemporary version was completed in 1994.

New Living Translation (NLT)

In 1971, Dr. Kenneth Taylor, founder of Tyndale House Publishers, completed a paraphrase of the entire Bible, which Tyndale published as *The Living Bible.* Later, this popular version was completely revised to create the New Living Translation. More than ninety evangelical scholars and theologians undertook the seven-year-long task of completing the NLT. The NLT remains true to the readability of *The Living Bible* yet is close to the Hebrew and Greek texts in meaning as well as style. The NLT was first published in 1996.

Perhaps the best way to choose the version that is right for you is simply to read the same passages in different versions and see which one appeals to you the most. I primarily use the New King James Version, although I incorporate many other translations in my study as well.

Even though the wording from one translation to another is slightly different, always remember that God protects His Word. The message is the same and it is still God's inspired Word. We can thank God for people like William Tyndale, who labored to bring the Word of God into English (and, in his case, gave his life for it), and for translators today who labor to make God's Word readable and accessible in hundreds of languages.

5

OVERVIEW OF THE BIBLE

The Bible is God's story of our salvation. It explains our basic problem (sin) and the solution that God has provided (sending Jesus to die on our behalf). If you keep the basic story in mind as you read, it will help you understand much of what God is saying through His Word.

At the end of this chapter, you will find a summary of each book of the Bible, including its author, the date it was written, the genre (or type of literature) it is, and a short summary of what the book contains. Let's take a journey through the Bible:

> The Bible is divided into the Old Testament and the New Testament. Of course, there was no OT [Old Testament] and NT [New Testament] before the coming of Christ, only one collection of sacred writings. But after the apostles and their associates produced another body of sacred literature, the church began to refer to the OT and NT. Actually "testament" is the Greek word that might better be rendered

"covenant." It denotes an arrangement made by God for the spiritual guidance and benefit of human beings. The covenant is unalterable: humankind may accept it or reject it but cannot change it. . . .

At least the first half of the OT follows a logical and easily understood arrangement. In Genesis through Esther the history of Israel from Abraham to the restoration [of Israel] appears largely in chronological order. Then follows a group of poetic books and the Major and Minor prophets ("Major" meaning the books that are relatively long; "Minor" meaning the books that are relatively short).

The NT also follows a generally logical arrangement. It begins with the four Gospels, which describe the birth, life, death, and resurrection of Christ and his training of disciples to carry on his work after his ascension. The book of Acts continues the narrative where the Gospels end and details the founding of the church and its spread through Mediterranean lands. In the latter part of the book the spotlight focuses on the apostle Paul and his church planting activities. Next come letters Paul addressed to churches he founded or to young ministers he tried to encourage. Following the Pauline epistles come a group commonly called the General Epistles [by other authors, such as Peter, James, and John]. The last book, Revelation, is an apocalyptic work.[5]

Revelation (literally "the unveiling") unlocks the "last days" scenario for us. It also is the only book of the Bible with a special blessing attached to the person who reads and keeps its words.

THE OLD TESTAMENT

Genesis

Writer: Moses

Date: 1450–1410 B.C.

Literary Style: Narrative

Genesis is the first book of the Bible. The word *genesis* means "the origin or coming into being of something." Recorded here are such important beginnings as the Creation, the fall of man, and the early years of the nation of Israel.

Familiar stories about people such as Abraham, Issac, Jacob, and Joseph are all found in this book.

Exodus

Writer: Moses

Date: 1450–1410 B.C.

Literary Style: Narrative

Exodus is about deliverance. The Israelites have moved to Egypt because of a famine. While there,

[5]Walter A. Elwell and Philip W. Comfort, eds., *Tyndale Bible Dictionary* (Wheaton, Ill.: 2001), 168.

they are made slaves. Because the Israelites are God's people, He appoints Moses to lead the Israelites out of Egypt and to the Promised Land, Canaan. On the way there, the Israelites stop at Mount Sinai, where God gives them the Ten Commandments.

Leviticus

Writer: Moses

Date: 1445–1444 B.C.

Literary Style: Law

Leviticus deals with the worship of a holy God. Here God gives the priests and people rules to live by to present themselves as holy before Him.

Numbers

Writer: Moses

Date: 1450–1410 B.C.

Literary Style: Narrative

Numbers takes its name from the two censuses (or "numberings") of the people recorded in this book. Yet Numbers is actually a sequel to Exodus. It follows the wanderings of the Israelites through the wilderness of Sinai for the next forty years until they camp just east of the Promised Land.

Deuteronomy

Writer: Moses

Date: 1407–1406 B.C.

Literary Style: Narrative

Deuteronomy is a farewell speech given to the

people of Israel by Moses just before his death. Moses knows that the people will face many new temptations as they move into the Promised Land. He knows they need to be reminded of God's promises to them and their responsibility to God and His laws.

Joshua

Writer: Joshua and possibly Phinehas

Date: Unknown

Literary Style: Narrative

Joshua is a book of conquest. Here the Israelites finally take possession of the Promised Land. The conquest is not immediate, though. It is a process of faith and action, through which God displays His miraculous power.

Judges

Writer: Probably Samuel

Date: Unknown

Literary Style: Narrative

This is a book about backsliding, defeat, and God's gracious deliverance. When the Israelites forget God, He allows them to be oppressed by a neighboring country. Then they cry out to God, and He raises up judges to deliver His people. The familiar story of the mighty Samson is found in this book.

Ruth

Writer: Unknown

Date: 1375–1050 B.C.

Literary Style: Narrative

The events of Ruth take place during some of the darkest days in the history of Israel. It is a time when the nation lapses again and again into the worship of false gods. In sharp contrast to this is the shining testimony of one Gentile woman from Moab who remains faithful to God.

1 Samuel

Writer: Samuel, Nathan, and Gad

Date: Unknown

Literary Style: Narrative

This book records a crucial time in Israel's history. Here the people of Israel reject God's chosen leader Samuel—a judge—and demand a king. Despite Samuel's warnings that a king will oppress them, the people insist that he anoint someone as king. So the leadership of Israel passes from Samuel to Saul, the nation's first king.

2 Samuel

Writer: Unknown

Date: 930 B.C.

Literary Style: Narrative

Second Samuel focuses on the life and career of Israel's greatest king—David. Under David, the kingdom of Israel doubles in size and its enemies are subdued. Though he is a good leader and popular with the people, David is not perfect. This book also records David's sin with Bathsheba and his tragic failure as a father.

1 Kings

Writer: Unknown

Date: Unknown

Literary Style: Narrative

In 1 Kings, David's reign comes to an end and his son Solomon becomes king. God gives Solomon the gift of wisdom and the blessing of building the temple. By the end of his reign, the kingdom is in an agitated state of unrest due to the excessive taxes for all of his building projects. The book ends as Solomon's son Rehoboam takes the throne, which leads to the division of the kingdom.

2 Kings

Writer: Unknown

Date: Unknown

Literary Style: Narrative

Second Kings shows the inability of God's people to rule themselves and the world. The kings of Israel and Judah turn their backs on God and lead their citizens astray. God sends many prophets to warn the people, but they refuse to listen. In the end, the kingdoms of Israel and Judah collapse, and their citizens are taken away into captivity.

1 Chronicles

Writer: Ezra

Date: 430 B.C.

Literary Style: Narrative

This book emphasizes the spiritual significance of

David's righteous reign. Through David's offspring will come the Messiah, Jesus Christ, whose throne and kingdom will be established forever.

2 Chronicles

Writer: Ezra

Date: 430 B.C.

Literary Style: Narrative

The emphasis in 2 Chronicles is on the southern kingdom, Judah, and on David's descendants. Here God uses five outstanding kings to bring periods of revival, renewal, and reformation to the land.

Ezra

Writer: Ezra

Date: 450 B.C.

Literary Style: Narrative

Ezra relates the account of the two returns from Babylon. It picks up where 2 Chronicles leaves off by showing how God fulfills His promise to bring His people back after seventy years of exile and captivity.

Nehemiah

Writer: Nehemiah

Date: 445–432 B.C.

Literary Style: Narrative

The book of Nehemiah is a wonderful story of how to handle opposition and discouragement when you are seeking to serve the Lord. Nehemiah is a cup-bearer for the king of Persia. After hearing about the danger the city of Jerusalem is in, he returns there and, despite local opposition, completes reconstruction of the walls and gates of the city in fifty-two days.

Esther

Writer: Unknown
Date: 483–471 B.C.
Literary Style: Narrative

The book of Esther shows God's providence at work in a profound way. As one Persian noble close to the king plots to kill the Jews, Esther, the Jewish queen, intercedes at great personal risk on behalf of her people.

Job

Writer: Possibly Job
Date: Unknown
Literary Style: Poetry

The book of Job addresses one of life's most-asked questions: Why does God allow suffering? Despite the fact that Job loses everything, suffers greatly, and has doubts about God, he remains faithful to God. In the end, God blesses him greatly.

Psalms

Writer: David, Asaph, the sons of Korah, Solomon, Heman, Ethan, and Moses
Date: 1440–586 B.C.
Literary Style: Poetry

The book of Psalms contains a variety of themes that

touch on every area of life. The central theme, however, is the praise and worship of a sovereign and loving God. Besides being a source of comfort and worship, the Psalms are filled with prophecies about Jesus Christ.

Proverbs

Writer: Solomon, Agur, and Lemuel

Date: Early in Solomon's reign

Literary Style: Wisdom Literature

Proverbs is a book of wisdom written by the wisest man who ever lived: Solomon. This book contains God's divine wisdom for every area of life, such as choosing friends, handling temptation, raising children, and knowing God.

Ecclesiastes

Writer: Solomon

Date: 935 B.C.

Literary Style: Wisdom Literature

Ecclesiastes is Solomon's analysis of life. Solomon has everything—incredible wealth, power, and intellect. He tries every enterprise and every pleasure known to man. Yet his final conclusion about life is that it is empty and purposeless without God.

Song of Songs

Writer: Solomon

Date: Unknown

Literary Style: Poetry

The Song of Songs is one of the most unusual

books in the Bible. On one level, it is an expression of pure love—as God intended it—in marriage. On another level, it symbolically speaks of God's love for His people and their love for Him.

Isaiah

Writer: Isaiah

Date: 700–681 B.C.

Literary Style: Prophecy

The book of Isaiah begins the prophetic portion of the Bible. It includes warnings of God's coming judgment upon the nations of Isaiah's day as well as prophecies about the future redeemer of humankind—Jesus Christ.

Jeremiah

Writer: Jeremiah

Date: 627–586 B.C.

Literary Style: Prophecy

Jeremiah is known as the weeping prophet. He delivers God's messages to the people of Judah. Although he passionately pleads with them to repent of their sins and return to God, the people ignore him and are taken into captivity in Babylon.

Lamentations

Writer: Jeremiah

Date: 586 B.C.

Literary Style: Poetry and Prophecy

Lamentations is a book of sadness. It opens with

Jeremiah weeping over the destruction of Jerusalem and the carting off of captives to Babylon. But near the end of the book, Jeremiah sees hope in the love and compassion of God.

Ezekiel

Writer: Ezekiel

Date: 571 B.C.

Literary Style: Prophecy

Ezekiel is taken captive to Babylon twelve years before the fall of Jerusalem in 586 B.C. While there, he is called by God to preach to the captives a message of judgment and salvation, to call them to repentance and obedience. The book of Ezekiel also contains dramatic prophecy about the regathering of the nation Israel in the scheme of last days events.

Daniel

Writer: Daniel

Date: 535 B.C.

Literary Style: Narrative and Prophecy

Like Ezekiel, Daniel is taken to Babylon in captivity, where he is trained to serve in the courts of the king. Through Daniel's writings, we learn of God's sovereignty and control of man's history. In addition, the book of Daniel contains some of the most well-known stories in the Bible, including Daniel in the lions' den and the three men in the fiery furnace. It is also a powerful prophetic book and should be read to understand the book of Revelation.

Hosea

Writer: Hosea

Date: 715 B.C.

Literary Style: Prophecy

Hosea is a tragic love story about God, who loves His people despite their unfaithfulness to Him. Hosea warns that one cannot disobey God without disastrous consequences. Yet this book dramatically portrays God's unending love and mercy as He offers forgiveness to those who repent.

Joel

Writer: Joel

Date: 835–796 B.C.

Literary Style: Prophecy

This book describes God's inescapable and overwhelming judgment upon sinful people. The prophet Joel is sent to warn the people of the coming judgment of God. He calls for the people to turn back to God before judgment falls upon them.

Amos

Writer: Amos

Date: 760–750 B.C.

Literary Style: Prophecy

Amos prophesies to the northern kingdom during a time of great prosperity. As a result of their prosperity, the people have become self-sufficient and indifferent toward God and others. Amos comes to warn them of the dangers of their indifference and spiritual complacency.

Obadiah

Writer: Obadiah
Date: Possibly 627–586 B.C.
Literary Style: Prophecy

The book of Obadiah demonstrates God's ongoing protection of His people from their enemies. As the Babylonians carry the Israelites off in captivity, the Edomites watch in indifference. Therefore, Obadiah lets them know that they will stand condemned and be destroyed while Israel will be restored.

Jonah

Writer: Jonah
Date: 785–760 B.C.
Literary Style: Narrative

This is the story of a man who tries to run from God and quickly learns the futility of it. After repenting of his sin, Jonah is restored and recommissioned. His preaching results in a large revival as the entire city of Nineveh turns to God.

Micah

Writer: Micah
Date: Possibly 742–687 B.C.
Literary Style: Prophecy

Micah gives us a glimpse of God's hatred of sin and, at the same time, his love for the sinner. This book also gives us some of the clearest predictions of the coming Messiah. Micah challenges us to live for God and join the faithful remnant of His people who live according to His will.

Nahum

Writer: Nahum

Date: 663–654 B.C.

Literary Style: Prophecy

Nahum teaches that God is the righteous judge and the supreme ruler over all. Those who continually do evil and oppress God's people, ignoring His repeated warnings, will pay a price.

Habakkuk

Writer: Habakkuk

Date: 612–589 B.C.

Literary Style: Prophecy

Habakkuk cannot understand how God can allow evil and injustice to persist in Judah. Yet as Habakkuk seeks God, he finds his answer in trusting God's character.

Zephaniah

Writer: Zephaniah

Date: 640–621 B.C.

Literary Style: Prophecy

Zephaniah preaches during a time of religious revival in Judah. But the religious zeal is shallow and inconsistent. The people rid their homes—but not their hearts—of idols. Zephaniah warns them that God does not take sin lightly and that He will punish those who sin.

Haggai

Writer: Haggai

Date: 520 B.C.

Literary Style: Prophecy

After some of the Jews return from captivity, they begin to rebuild the destroyed temple. But due to opposition and spiritual apathy, they stop construction. Haggai calls the Jews to finish the temple. He encourages the people to wake up from their apathy and reorder their priorities, putting God first in their lives.

Zechariah

Writer: Zechariah
Date: 520–480 B.C.
Literary Style: Prophecy

Zechariah ministers with Haggai during the rebuilding of the temple. He brings God's message of encouragement and hope to a discouraged people.

Malachi

Writer: Malachi
Date: 430 B.C.
Literary Style: Prophecy

The book of Malachi is a beautiful expression of God's mercy and grace to a nation so unworthy of either. Israel, God's chosen people, willfully disobeys God. Yet like a father pleading with his children, God extends a hand of forgiveness to those who turn and faithfully follow after Him.

THE NEW TESTAMENT

Matthew

Writer: Matthew (Levi)

Date: A.D. 60–65

Literary Style: Gospel

Matthew writes his Gospel with the Jew in mind and therefore includes many references to Old Testament prophecies that Jesus fulfills. It contains at least 129 quotations from or allusions to the Old Testament. Matthew's objective is to show the Jewish people that Jesus is indeed their long-awaited Messiah.

Mark

Writer: John Mark

Date: A.D. 55–65

Literary Style: Gospel

The Gospel of Mark is the account of the life, ministry, miracles, and words of Jesus Christ. In contrast to Matthew, who primarily presents Jesus as the Messiah, Mark emphasizes the servanthood of the Lord.

Luke

Writer: Luke

Date: A.D. 60

Literary Style: Gospel

Luke is a Gentile who put his faith in Jesus Christ. His purpose for writing an account of Jesus Christ's life, death, and resurrection is to make the message of salvation understandable to those outside the Jewish faith and culture.

John

Writer: John
Date: A.D. 85–90
Literary Style: Gospel

While the emphasis in the other three Gospels centers around the events in the life of Jesus, John often focuses upon the meaning of those events. For instance, while all four Gospels record the miracle of the feeding of the five thousand, only John gives us Jesus' message on the "Bread of Life," which follows that miracle. John writes this Gospel so that people might believe, and he puts special emphasis on the deity of Jesus Christ.

Acts

Writer: Luke
Date: A.D. 63–70
Literary Style: History

This book shows the church's early development and rapid growth. It reveals how the dynamic power of the Holy Spirit transforms a diverse group of fishermen, tax collectors, and other ordinary folks into people who turn their world upside down with the gospel of Jesus Christ.

Romans

Writer: Paul
Date: A.D. 70
Literary Style: Epistle (letter)

This letter to the church at Rome contains some of the prime secrets of the Christian life. It is a hard-hitting diagnosis of the primary source of people's problems—sin. It also shows the futility of thinking that the answers to our problems lie within ourselves. It is a foundational book that must be carefully studied by every Christian.

1 Corinthians

Writer: Paul

Date: A.D. 55

Literary Style: Epistle

Paul writes this epistle in response to certain situations that have arisen in the Corinthian church. He straightforwardly deals with many of the errors that the people of this church believe and practice. Among these pitfalls are sins of immorality, false teachings, and problems regarding marriage and lawsuits. This book contains foundational teaching on the proper use of the gifts of the Spirit.

2 Corinthians

Writer: Paul

Date: A.D. 55–57

Literary Style: Epistle

Some of the Corinthians still living in sin after Paul's first letter have begun to deny Paul's authority. Paul writes this second letter to deal with the problems that persist within the Corinthian church.

Galatians

Writer: Paul

Date: A.D. 49

Literary Style: Epistle

Galatians is a foundational study that shows how complete the work of Jesus' death on the cross is for our salvation. Nothing needs to be added to that work—nor does it need to be improved upon—for you can't improve upon perfection.

Ephesians

Writer: Paul

Date: A.D. 60

Literary Style: Epistle

The book of Ephesians shows us our rightful position as children of God "in the heavenlies" with Jesus Christ. It tells us of all that God has done for us, as well as how to fully appreciate and implement it practically in our lives. This book also contains essential teaching on spiritual warfare and the Christian family.

Philippians

Writer: Paul

Date: A.D. 61

Literary Style: Epistle

This book explains the mind-set, attitude, and outlook the believer must have if he or she is going to experience the joy of the Lord in a troubled world.

Colossians

Writer: Paul

Date: A.D. 60

Literary Style: Epistle

Paul writes this epistle to refute certain false teachings that have found their way into the church at Colosse. A common theme of this book is the superiority of Jesus Christ.

1 Thessalonians

Writer: Paul

Date: A.D. 51

Literary Style: Epistle

The theme of this letter focuses upon living a godly and holy life as we await the return of Jesus Christ. Paul also offers words of comfort concerning Christian loved ones who have died.

2 Thessalonians

Writer: Paul

Date: A.D. 51

Literary Style: Epistle

This letter offers encouragement to believers who are facing persecution. It also offers correct teaching on the subject of "the day of the Lord," a confusing matter for some of the Thessalonian believers. In addition, some Thessalonians are not living as they should in light of the return of the Lord, so Paul addresses that issue as well.

1 Timothy

Writer: Paul

Date: A.D. 64

Literary Style: Epistle

Paul, under the inspiration of the Holy Spirit, lays out what the conduct of the church and its leaders should be. Though Timothy himself is a pastor, these words apply to all who want to be used by God and have their lives make a difference.

2 Timothy

Writer: Paul

Date: A.D. 67

Literary Style: Epistle

Paul writes this second letter to Timothy to encourage him to be faithful to Christ. Paul also includes a glimpse of what the last days will look like. This is the final epistle that Paul writes before his death.

Titus

Writer: Paul

Date: A.D. 65

Literary Style: Epistle

Paul writes this letter to address the challenges facing Titus as an overseer of the churches on the island of Crete. He includes criteria for qualifications of leadership, sound teaching, and good works.

Philemon

Writer: Paul

Date: A.D. 60

Literary Style: Epistle

This short but profound epistle contains a wonderful story of the importance of forgiveness among
Christians.

Hebrews

Writer: Unknown

Date: A.D. 68

Literary Style: Epistle

The book of Hebrews is written for Jews who have
accepted Jesus as their Messiah. It warns them of the
danger of slipping back into the traditions of Judaism
because they have not put their roots down in the soil
of Christianity.

James

Writer: James, Jesus' half-brother

Date: A.D. 49

Literary Style: Epistle

James speaks a lot about faith in his book, with an
emphasis on results. He stresses the need to live a
practical, seven-days-a-week, working faith.

1 Peter

Writer: Peter

Date: A.D. 65

Literary Style: Epistle

The theme of Peter's first epistle is suffering. He
brings inspired words of comfort to those who suffer
under persecution.

2 Peter

Writer: Peter
Date: A.D. 66
Literary Style: Epistle

In this epistle Peter reminds the believers of certain important spiritual truths. Peter also warns of false teachers and speaks of the hope of the coming of the Lord.

1 John

Writer: John
Date: A.D. 90–95
Literary Style: Epistle

In this letter John points out that a person either is or is not a child of God. There is no middle ground. John clearly emphasizes that if one is really a child of God, it is evident in one's outward behavior.

2 John

Writer: John
Date: A.D. 90–95
Literary Style: Epistle

In this letter John points out that true Christian love involves more than just an emotional feeling. It is grounded in what is true. John also warns of false teachers, urging believers not to receive them.

3 John

Writer: John
Date: A.D. 90–95

Literary Style: Epistle

John writes this letter to commend a believer named Gaius for the hospitality he shows to traveling teachers of the gospel.

Jude

Writer: Jude, Jesus' half-brother

Date: A.D. 65

Literary Style: Epistle

The book of Jude is one of the shortest books in the New Testament. Its theme centers around the great apostasy, or falling away from the faith, that will happen on earth before the return of Jesus Christ.

Revelation

Writer: John

Date: A.D. 95

Literary Style: Apocalyptic

In this great book we learn of the return of Jesus Christ to the earth, as well as the events preceding that climactic moment. Again, it is the only book of the Bible that promises a special blessing to the person who hears and keeps its truths.

52 Great Bible Stories

The following list not only gives you the fifty-two Bible stories you should be familiar with as a Christian, it provides an
interesting reading plan as well. Using the list below, you can
read through one great Bible story a week for a whole year.

1. In the Beginning GENESIS 1:1–2:4

In an incredible display of majesty and power, God cre-
ates the heavens and the earth and everything in them.

2. The First Sin GENESIS 2:5–3:24

God's original plan for humankind is spoiled in one
small but deliberate act of disobedience that enables sin
to enter the human race.

3. Noah and the Ark GENESIS 6:1–9:17

One man's faith in and obedience to God spares his
family from certain death in the greatest flood ever experienced by humankind.

4. Sodom and Gomorrah GENESIS 18:16–19:29

Lot, a God-fearing man, allows outside influences and
selfish pursuits to cloud his thinking. Though he es-
capes the destruction of his evil hometown, his com-
promising decisions leave a devastating mark on his life
and family.

5. Abraham and Isaac GENESIS 22:1-18

Abraham learns that complete obedience can mean
great sacrifice—but also great blessing.

6. The Story of Joseph GENESIS 37:1-36; 39:1–45:28

Despite his virtuous lifestyle and his love for God, nothing seems to go right for Joseph. Yet Joseph's personal faith empowers him to rise above his trials and temptations, and he ultimately finds strength and blessing in spite of his hardships.

7. The Burning Bush EXODUS 3:1–4:17

While tending sheep in the desert, Moses sees an unusual sight that leads him into a personal encounter with the living God.

8. The Ten Plagues EXODUS 7:14–12:30

Pharaoh refuses to let the Israelites leave Egypt. To convince Pharaoh to change his mind, God sends a series of plagues. Unfortunately, Pharaoh's pride ends up costing him something precious—the life of his firstborn son.

9. The Great Escape EXODUS 12:31–14:31

Moses and the Israelites overcome tremendous obstacles and learn the importance of completely trusting in God as they make their way to the Promised Land.

10. The Twelve Scouts and Their Report NUMBERS 13:1–14:45

When Caleb and Joshua choose to follow God's orders despite popular opinion, they appear to be in trouble. God, however, turns the tables in their favor.

11. Balaam and the Talking Donkey NUMBERS 22:21-35

Balaam tests God by going against His will—for profit. Fortunately, Balaam's donkey saves him from God's wrath.

12. The Battle of Jericho JOSHUA 5:13–6:27

Marching and music play a strategic role in this unusual battle plan. Nevertheless, when the Israelites follow God's orders, they win a mighty victory. This story shows faith in action.

13. The Story of Gideon and His Army JUDGES 6:1–7:25

Gideon feels completely unfit for God's service, yet he
learns how much God can accomplish with very little.

14. The Rise and Fall of Samson JUDGES 13:1–16:31

God wants to use Samson for His purposes, but Samson
allows pride and lust to ruin his potential. He is a "heman" with a "she-weakness." In spite of Samson's disobedience, God still extends grace to him in the end.

15. The Story of Ruth RUTH 1:1–4:22

Ruth, young and widowed, chooses to leave her home for
an unknown land and an uncertain future in order to
care for her mother-in-law and worship the one true
God. God blesses Ruth for her tender faith in a profound
and special way.

16. The Calling of Samuel 1 SAMUEL 1:1–3:21

God uses the most unlikely person, a small child, to deliver a devastating message to Eli the priest.

17. David and Goliath 1 SAMUEL 17:1-58

David overcomes seemingly insurmountable odds and
silences his skeptics when he kills Goliath, the mighty
Philistine warrior, with a few small stones and an un-
shakable faith in God.

18. True Friends 1 SAMUEL 20:1-42

David and Jonathan overcome tremendous odds to become the best of friends.

19. David Sins with Bathsheba 2 SAMUEL 11:1–12:25

David underestimates his potential to fall when he allows lust to control his thoughts. He soon discovers that
one act of passion can lead to a lifetime of regret.

20. Elijah and the Prophets of Baal 1 KINGS 18:16-40

The prophet Elijah puts his faith on the line when he

challenges the religious leaders of a pagan deity to match the mighty work of his God.

21. Naaman the Leper 2 KINGS 5:1-27

A servant girl tells Naaman's wife about a prophet in Israel who can heal Naaman of his leprosy. With hope, the great commander Naaman looks for the prophet—Elisha—to heal him. But what Elisha tells Naaman to do requires faith.

22. Lepers Discover an Abandoned Camp 2 KINGS 7:3-16

In desperation, four starving lepers leave the safety of Samaria's gates to surrender to the enemy army that has besieged the city. Hoping to be fed, the lepers discover something even better.

23. Hezekiah's Illness 2 KINGS 20:1-11

On his deathbed, Hezekiah, the king of Judah, prays to the Lord asking Him to remember his faithfulness and devotion. In an incredible act of mercy, God spares Hezekiah's life and even adds fifteen years to it.

24. Jehoshaphat Defeats Moab and Ammon

2 CHRONICLES 20:1-30

Jehoshaphat leans upon the Lord and His wisdom when faced with a great battle—and Jehoshaphat wins overwhelmingly.

25. Nehemiah Rebuilds the Wall NEHEMIAH 1:1-7:3

One man's faith helps him persevere through adversity and accomplish a great task.

26. The Story of Queen Esther ESTHER 1:1-10:3

Queen Esther has it all, yet she is willing to give up everything in order to obey God and save her people, the Jews.

27. The Story of Shadrach, Meshach, and Abednego

DANIEL 3:1-30

These three men refuse to follow orders that contradict

God's law. In the end, their uncompromising stance changes the heart of a selfish tyrant.

28. Daniel in the Lions' Den DANIEL 6:1-28
Daniel takes his faith so seriously that he does not fear when it leads to persecution. He realizes that God is ultimately in control—even in a lions' den.

29. Jonah and the Great Fish JONAH 1:1–4:11
Jonah finds that it does not pay to run away from God and His plan for your life.

30. Jesus' Birth MATTHEW 1:18-25; LUKE 1:26-38; 2:1-7
In the most humble and amazing circumstances, the Savior of the world is born.

31. Jesus Visits the Temple As a Boy LUKE 2:41-52
As Jesus' parents return home from the Passover feast in Jerusalem, they notice that Jesus is not with them. Where they find Him and what they find Him doing astonishes them.

32. Jesus' Baptism MATTHEW 3:13-17; MARK 1:9-11; LUKE 3:21-22
At Jesus' baptism, God expresses His pleasure in His Son and calls Him to public ministry.

33. Satan Tempts Jesus
MATTHEW 4:1-11; MARK 1:12-13; LUKE 4:1-13
Jesus withstands temptation from the devil himself, giving His followers a model to follow when they encounter temptation.

34. Jesus Clears the Temple
MATTHEW 21:12-17; MARK 11:15-19; LUKE 19:45-48
In one bold act, Jesus shows His zeal for God's house, making bitter enemies in the process.

35. Jesus and the Miraculous Catch of Fish LUKE 5:1-11
Jesus' disciples reap great dividends when they follow Jesus' unusual advice.

36. Jesus and the Samaritan Woman   JOHN 4:1-30

A woman who has spent her life looking for love finds true fulfillment and joy in Jesus Christ.

37. Jesus Calms the Storm at Sea

MATTHEW 8:23-27; MARK 4:35-41; LUKE 8:22-25

The disciples discover that although life can be unpredictable, Jesus can calm the storms.

38. Jesus Heals a Lame Man   JOHN 5:1-15

A lame man who has been waiting for healing for more than thirty years receives immediate healing when he follows Jesus' instructions.

39. Jesus Feeds Five Thousand

MATTHEW 14:13-21; MARK 6:30-44; LUKE 9:10-17; JOHN 6:1-14

A little boy's lunch becomes the focal point of one of Jesus' greatest recorded miracles.

40. The Parable of the Good Samaritan   LUKE 10:25-37

The person we should consider to be our neighbor or friend may not be the person we expect, as this parable explains.

41. Jesus Heals a Blind Man   JOHN 9:1-41

This man not only receives his physical sight but also his spiritual sight as he sees Jesus for who He is.

42. Jesus Raises Lazarus from the Dead   JOHN 11:1-44

While Lazarus's sisters expect Jesus to perform a healing, Jesus chooses to do something far greater.

43. The Prodigal Son   LUKE 15:11-32

Jesus illustrates God's mercy and forgiveness in this parable of a wayward son, and He shows us how to get right with God.

44. Zacchaeus Climbs a Sycamore Tree   LUKE 19:1-10

A lonely and despised man finds love and forgiveness in Jesus.

45. The Last Supper

MATTHEW 26:20-30; MARK 14:17-26; LUKE 22:14-30; JOHN 13:1-30

Jesus uses some of His last moments with His disciples to teach them important lessons about servanthood and the meaning of His impending sacrifice.

46. Jesus' Crucifixion

MATTHEW 27:15-66; MARK 15:2-47; LUKE 23:1-56; JOHN 18:28–19:42

The Son of God shows His tremendous love for people by enduring the most humiliating torture and execution befitting the worst criminal.

47. Jesus' Resurrection

MATTHEW 28:1-10; MARK 16:1-8; LUKE 24:1-12; JOHN 20:1-18

Christ's death seems to be a hopeless situation. But what His followers do not know is that He will rise from the dead and break sin's hold on humankind.

48. Peter's First Sermon ACTS 2:14-41

A once dejected and disloyal follower, Peter shows his love for Jesus by preaching a powerful sermon through which many come to faith in Christ.

49. Saul's Conversion ACTS 9:1-19

One of the earliest persecutors of Christians becomes a believer while he is on his way to arrest Christians in Damascus.

50. An Angel Rescues Peter from Prison ACTS 12:1-19

A prayer meeting receives a dramatic answer in the middle of the night.

51. Paul and Silas in Prison ACTS 16:16-40

Paul and Silas rise above their circumstances by praising God for His goodness through their trials.

52. Paul's Journey to Rome ACTS 27:1–28:16

A seemingly hopeless situation turns into a tremendous witnessing opportunity for the apostle Paul.

Through the New Testament in a Year

January 1
Matthew 1:1-17
Romans 1:1-7

January 2
Matthew 1:18-25
Romans 1:8-15

January 3
Matthew 2:1-12
Romans 1:16-17

January 4
Matthew 2:13-23
Romans 1:18-32

January 5
Matthew 3:1-12
Romans 2:1-16

January 6
Matthew 3:13-17
Romans 2:17-29

January 7
Matthew 4:1-11
Romans 3:1-8

January 8
Matthew 4:12-25
Romans 3:9-20

January 9
Matthew 5:1-16
Romans 3:21-31

January 10
Matthew 5:17-48
Romans 4:1-12

January 11
Matthew 6:1-18
Romans 4:13-17

January 12
Matthew 6:19-34
Romans 4:18-25

January 13
Matthew 7:1-6
Romans 5:1-5

January 14
Matthew 7:7-12
Romans 5:6-11

January 15
Matthew 7:13-29
Romans 5:12-21

January 16
Matthew 8:1-17
Romans 6:1-14

January 17
  Matthew 8:18-22
  Romans 6:15-23

January 18
  Matthew 8:23-34
  Romans 7:1-6

January 19
  Matthew 9:1-8
  Romans 7:7-13

January 20
  Matthew 9:9-13
  Romans 7:14-25

January 21
  Matthew 9:14-17
  Romans 8:1-8

January 22
  Matthew 9:18-26
  Romans 8:9-17

January 23
  Matthew 9:27-38
  Romans 8:18-27

January 24
  Matthew 10:1-18
  Romans 8:28-39

January 25
  Matthew 10:19–11:1
  Romans 9:1-5

January 26
  Matthew 11:2-19
  Romans 9:6-18

January 27
  Matthew 11:20-30
  Romans 9:19-26

January 28
  Matthew 12:1-21
  Romans 9:27-33

January 29
  Matthew 12:22-37
  Romans 10:1-13

January 30
  Matthew 12:38-50
  Romans 10:14-21

January 31
  Matthew 13:1-23
  Romans 11:1-6

February 1
  Matthew 13:24-35
  Romans 11:7-12

February 2
  Matthew 13:36-43
  Romans 11:13-21

February 3
  Matthew 13:44-58
  Romans 11:22-27

February 4
  Matthew 14:1-12
  Romans 11:28-36

February 5
Matthew 14:13-21
Romans 12:1-5

February 6
Matthew 14:22-36
Romans 12:6-13

February 7
Matthew 15:1-20
Romans 12:14-21

February 8
Matthew 15:21-28
Romans 13:1-7

February 9
Matthew 15:29-39
Romans 13:8-14

February 10
Matthew 16:1-12
Romans 14:1-4

February 11
Matthew 16:13-28
Romans 14:5-9

February 12
Matthew 17:1-13
Romans 14:10-16

February 13
Matthew 17:14-21
Romans 14:17-23

February 14
Matthew 17:22-27
Romans 15:1-6

February 15
Matthew 18:1-20
Romans 15:7-17

February 16
Matthew 18:21-35
Romans 15:18-22

February 17
Matthew 19:1-12
Romans 15:23-33

February 18
Matthew 19:13-15
Romans 16:1-16

February 19
Matthew 19:16-30
Romans 16:17-27

February 20
Matthew 20:1-19
1 Corinthians 1:1-9

February 21
Matthew 20:20-28
1 Corinthians 1:10-17

February 22
Matthew 20:29-34
1 Corinthians 1:18-25

February 23
Matthew 21:1-17
1 Corinthians 1:26-31

February 24
Matthew 21:18-22
1 Corinthians 2:1-10

February 25
Matthew 21:23-46
1 Corinthians 2:11-16

February 26
Matthew 22:1-14
1 Corinthians 3:1-9

February 27
Matthew 22:15-46
1 Corinthians 3:10-17

February 28
Matthew 23:1-12
1 Corinthians 3:18-23

March 1
Matthew 23:13-39
1 Corinthians 4:1-7

March 2
Matthew 24:1-31
1 Corinthians 4:8-13

March 3
Matthew 24:32-51
1 Corinthians 4:14-21

March 4
Matthew 25:1-13
1 Corinthians 5:1-8

March 5
Matthew 25:14-30
1 Corinthians 5:9-13

March 6
Matthew 25:31-46
1 Corinthians 6:1-8

March 7
Matthew 26:1-16
1 Corinthians 6:9-13

March 8
Matthew 26:17-35
1 Corinthians 6:14-20

March 9
Matthew 26:36-56
1 Corinthians 7:1-9

March 10
Matthew 26:57-75
1 Corinthians 7:10-17

March 11
Matthew 27:1-10
1 Corinthians 7:18-24

March 12
Matthew 27:11-30
1 Corinthians 7:25-31

March 13
Matthew 27:31-56
1 Corinthians 7:32-40

March 14
Matthew 27:57-66
1 Corinthians 8:1-13

March 15
Matthew 28:1-15
1 Corinthians 9:1-10

March 16
Matthew 28:16-20
1 Corinthians 9:11-18

March 17
Mark 1:1-8
1 Corinthians 9:19 27

March 18
Mark 1:9-13
1 Corinthians 10:1-14

March 19
Mark 1:14-20
1 Corinthians 10:15-22

March 20
Mark 1:21-28
1 Corinthians 10:23–11:1

March 21
Mark 1:29-39
1 Corinthians 11:2-16

March 22
Mark 1:40-45
1 Corinthians 11:17-22

March 23
Mark 2:1-12
1 Corinthians 11:23-34

March 24
Mark 2:13-17
1 Corinthians 12:1-3

March 25
Mark 2:18-22
1 Corinthians 12:4-11

March 26
Mark 2:23–3:6
1 Corinthians 12:12-18

March 27
Mark 3:7-19
1 Corinthians 12:19-27

March 28
Mark 3:20-35
1 Corinthians 12:28-31

March 29
Mark 4:1-20
1 Corinthians 13:1-7

March 30
Mark 4:21-34
1 Corinthians 13:8-13

March 31
Mark 4:35-41
1 Corinthians 14:1-5

April 1
Mark 5:1-20
1 Corinthians 14:6-12

April 2
Mark 5:21-43
1 Corinthians 14:13-17

April 3
Mark 6:1-6
1 Corinthians 14:18-25

April 4
Mark 6:7-13
1 Corinthians 14:26-32

April 5
Mark 6:14-29
1 Corinthians 14:33-40

April 6
Mark 6:30-44
1 Corinthians 15:1-11

April 7
Mark 6:45-56
1 Corinthians 15:12-20

April 8
Mark 7:1-23
1 Corinthians 15:21-28

April 9
Mark 7:24-37
1 Corinthians 15:29-34

April 10
Mark 8:1-10
1 Corinthians 15:35-44

April 11
Mark 8:11-21
1 Corinthians 15:45-49

April 12
Mark 8:22-26
1 Corinthians 15:50-58

April 13
Mark 8:27-38
1 Corinthians 16:1-9

April 14
Mark 9:1-13
1 Corinthians 16:10-18

April 15
Mark 9:14-29
1 Corinthians 16:19-24

April 16
Mark 9:30-37
2 Corinthians 1:1-7

April 17
Mark 9:38-50
2 Corinthians 1:8-14

April 18
Mark 10:1-12
2 Corinthians 1:15-24

April 19
Mark 10:13-16
2 Corinthians 2:1-4

April 20
Mark 10:17-31
2 Corinthians 2:5-11

April 21
Mark 10:32-45
2 Corinthians 2:12-17

April 22
Mark 10:46-52
2 Corinthians 3:1-6

April 23
Mark 11:1-11
2 Corinthians 3:7-18

April 24
Mark 11:12-27
2 Corinthians 4:1-7

April 25
Mark 11:28–12:12
2 Corinthians 4:8-17

April 26
Mark 12:13-34
2 Corinthians 4:18–5:10

April 27
Mark 12:35-44
2 Corinthians 5:11-21

April 28
Mark 13:1-13
2 Corinthians 6:1-7

April 29
Mark 13:14-37
2 Corinthians 6:8-13

April 30
Mark 14:1-11
2 Corinthians 6:14–7:4

May 1
Mark 14:12-31
2 Corinthians 7:5-10

May 2
Mark 14:32-52
2 Corinthians 7:11-16

May 3
Mark 14:53-72
2 Corinthians 8:1-8

May 4
Mark 15:1-20
2 Corinthians 8:9-15

May 5
Mark 15:21-32
2 Corinthians 8:16-24

May 6
Mark 15:33-47
2 Corinthians 9:1-5

May 7
Mark 16:1-20
2 Corinthians 9:6-15

May 8
Luke 1:1-25
2 Corinthians 10:1-6

May 9
Luke 1:26-56
2 Corinthians 10:7-12

May 10
Luke 1:57-80
2 Corinthians 10:13-18

May 11
Luke 2:1-20
2 Corinthians 11:1-6

May 12
Luke 2:21-40
2 Corinthians 11:7-15

May 13
  Luke 2:41-52
  2 Corinthians 11:16-33

May 14
  Luke 3:1-18
  2 Corinthians 12:1-10

May 15
  Luke 3:19-23a
  2 Corinthians 12:11-15

May 16
  Luke 3:23b-38
  2 Corinthians 12:16-21

May 17
  Luke 4:1-13
  2 Corinthians 13:1-6

May 18
  Luke 4:14-30
  2 Corinthians 13:7-14

May 19
  Luke 4:31-44
  Galatians 1:1-5

May 20
  Luke 5:1-11
  Galatians 1:6-12

May 21
  Luke 5:12-16
  Galatians 1:13-24

May 22
  Luke 5:17-26
  Galatians 2:1-5

May 23
  Luke 5:27-39
  Galatians 2:6-10

May 24
  Luke 6:1-11
  Galatians 2:11-16

May 25
  Luke 6:12-16
  Galatians 2:17-21

May 26
  Luke 6:17-38
  Galatians 3:1-9

May 27
  Luke 6:39-49
  Galatians 3:10-14

May 28
  Luke 7:1-10
  Galatians 3:15-20

May 29
  Luke 7:11-17
  Galatians 3:21-29

May 30
  Luke 7:18-35
  Galatians 4:1-7

May 31
  Luke 7:36-50
  Galatians 4:8-11

June 21
  Luke 11:29-36
  Ephesians 4:25-32

June 22
  Luke 11:37-54
  Ephesians 5:1-9

June 23
  Luke 12:1-12
  Ephesians 5:10-20

June 24
  Luke 12:13-34
  Ephesians 5:21-33

June 25
  Luke 12:35-48
  Ephesians 6:1-4

June 26
  Luke 12:49-59
  Ephesians 6:5-9

June 27
  Luke 13:1-9
  Ephesians 6:10-17

June 28
  Luke 13:10-17
  Ephesians 6:18-24

June 29
  Luke 13:18-21
  Philippians 1:1-6

June 30
  Luke 13:22-30
  Philippians 1:7-11

July 1
  Luke 13:31-35
  Philippians 1:12-18a

July 2
  Luke 14:1-6
  Philippians 1:18b-30

July 3
  Luke 14:7-24
  Philippians 2:1-11

July 4
  Luke 14:25-35
  Philippians 2:12-18

July 5
  Luke 15:1-10
  Philippians 2:19-30

July 6
  Luke 15:11-32
  Philippians 3:1-7

July 7
  Luke 16:1-14
  Philippians 3:8-12

July 8
  Luke 16:15-31
  Philippians 3:13-16

July 9
  Luke 17:1-4
  Philippians 3:17-21

July 10
Luke 17:5-10
Philippians 4:1-7

July 11
Luke 17:11-19
Philippians 4:8-14

July 12
Luke 17:20-37
Philippians 4:15-23

July 13
Luke 18:1-8
Colossians 1:1-6

July 14
Luke 18:9-17
Colossians 1:7-9

July 15
Luke 18:18-30
Colossians 1:10-14

July 16
Luke 18:31-34
Colossians 1:15-18

July 17
Luke 18:35-43
Colossians 1:19-23

July 18
Luke 19:1-10
Colossians 1:24-29

July 19
Luke 19:11-27
Colossians 2:1-10

July 20
Luke 19:28-40
Colossians 2:11-15

July 21
Luke 19:41-48
Colossians 2:16-23

July 22
Luke 20:1-19
Colossians 3:1-8

July 23
Luke 20:20-26
Colossians 3:9-14

July 24
Luke 20:27-47
Colossians 3:15-17

July 25
Luke 21:1-4
Colossians 3:18–4:1

July 26
Luke 21:5-19
Colossians 4:2-6

July 27
Luke 21:20-38
Colossians 4:7-18

July 28
Luke 22:1-23
1 Thessalonians 1:1-10

July 29
Luke 22:24-30
1 Thessalonians 2:1-8

July 30
Luke 22:31-34
1 Thessalonians 2:9-13

July 31
Luke 22:35-38
1 Thessalonians 2:14—3:4

August 1
Luke 22:39-53
1 Thessalonians 3:5-8

August 2
Luke 22:54-62
1 Thessalonians 3:9-13

August 3
Luke 22:63-71
1 Thessalonians 4:1-8

August 4
Luke 23:1-25
1 Thessalonians 4:9-12

August 5
Luke 23:26-43
1 Thessalonians 4:13—5:3

August 6
Luke 23:44-56
1 Thessalonians 5:4-11

August 7
Luke 24:1-12
1 Thessalonians 5:12-22

August 8
Luke 24:13-34
1 Thessalonians 5:23-28

August 9
Luke 24:35-53
2 Thessalonians 1:1-12

August 10
John 1:1-14
2 Thessalonians 2:1-6

August 11
John 1:15-34
2 Thessalonians 2:7-17

August 12
John 1:35-51
2 Thessalonians 3:1-5

August 13
John 2:1-12
2 Thessalonians 3:6-18

August 14
John 2:13-25
1 Timothy 1:1-6

August 15
John 3:1-21
1 Timothy 1:7-11

August 16
John 3:22-36
1 Timothy 1:12-17

August 17
John 4:1-30
1 Timothy 1:18-20

September 6
John 11:30-46
2 Timothy 2:15-21

September 7
John 11:47-57
2 Timothy 2:22-26

September 8
John 12:1-11
2 Timothy 3:1-9

September 9
John 12:12-19
2 Timothy 3:10-17

September 10
John 12:20-36
2 Timothy 4:1-4

September 11
John 12:37-50
2 Timothy 4:5-8

September 12
John 13:1-20
2 Timothy 4:9-22

September 13
John 13:21-38
Titus 1:1-5

September 14
John 14:1-14
Titus 1:6-16

September 15
John 14:15-31
Titus 2:1-10

September 16
John 15:1-15
Titus 2:11-15

September 17
John 15:16-27
Titus 3:1-8

September 18
John 16:1-15
Titus 3:9-15

September 19
John 16:16-33
Philemon 1:1-7

September 20
John 17:1-26
Philemon 1:8-25

September 21
John 18:1-14
Hebrews 1:1-14

September 22
John 18:15-27
Hebrews 2:1-4

September 23
John 18:28-40
Hebrews 2:5-10

September 24
John 19:1-15
Hebrews 2:11-15

September 25
John 19:16-30
Hebrews 2:16–3:6

October 15
Acts 7:44-60
Hebrews 10:1-10

October 16
Acts 8:1-25
Hebrews 10:11-22

October 17
Acts 8:26-40
Hebrews 10:23-25

October 18
Acts 9:1-19a
Hebrews 10:26-31

October 19
Acts 9:19b-31
Hebrews 10:32-39

October 20
Acts 9:32-35
Hebrews 11:1-6

October 21
Acts 9:36-43
Hebrews 11:7-12

October 22
Acts 10:1-23a
Hebrews 11:13-16

October 23
Acts 10:23b-48
Hebrews 11:17-20

October 24
Acts 11:1-18
Hebrews 11:21-23

October 25
Acts 11:19-30
Hebrews 11:24-29

October 26
Acts 12:1-25
Hebrews 11:30-40

October 27
Acts 13:1-12
Hebrews 12:1-4

October 28
Acts 13:13-23
Hebrews 12:5-11

October 29
Acts 13:24-44
Hebrews 12:12-17

October 30
Acts 13:45-52
Hebrews 12:18-24

October 31
Acts 14:1-7
Hebrews 12:25-29

November 1
Acts 14:8-20a
Hebrews 13:1-9

November 2
Acts 14:20b-28
Hebrews 13:10-16

November 23
Acts 23:12-35
1 Peter 2:1-10

November 24
Acts 24:1-9
1 Peter 2:11-16

November 25
Acts 24:10-27
1 Peter 2:17-25

November 26
Acts 25:1-12
1 Peter 3:1-6

November 27
Acts 25:13-27
1 Peter 3:7-9

November 28
Acts 26:1-32
1 Peter 3:10-16

November 29
Acts 27:1-15
1 Peter 3:17-22

November 30
Acts 27:16-44
1 Peter 4:1-6

December 1
Acts 28:1-10
1 Peter 4:7-11

December 2
Acts 28:11-31
1 Peter 4:12-19

December 3
Revelation 1:1-8
1 Peter 5:1-7

December 4
Revelation 1:9-20
1 Peter 5:8-14

December 5
Revelation 2:1-7
2 Peter 1:1-11

December 6
Revelation 2:8-11
2 Peter 1:12-18

December 7
Revelation 2:12-17
2 Peter 1:19–2:11

December 8
Revelation 2:18-29
2 Peter 2:12-22

December 9
Revelation 3:1-6
2 Peter 3:1-7

December 10
Revelation 3:7-13
2 Peter 3:8-13

December 11
Revelation 3:14-22
2 Peter 3:14-18